YOUR KNOWLEDGE HAS VALUE

Martin Ruppe

Potential and Limits of Outsourcing Procurement

E-Procurement at BMW Group and Daimler Chrysler AG

GRIN Publishing

Bibliographic information published by the German National Library:

The German National Library lists this publication in the National Bibliography; detailed bibliographic data are available on the Internet at http://dnb.dnb.de .

Imprint:

Copyright © 2014 GRIN Verlag GmbH
Print and binding: Books on Demand GmbH, Norderstedt Germany
ISBN: 978-3-656-68075-8

This book at GRIN:

http://www.grin.com/en/e-book/275426/potential-and-limits-of-outsourcing-procurement

GRIN - Your knowledge has value

Since its foundation in 1998, GRIN has specialized in publishing academic texts by students, college teachers and other academics as e-book and printed book. The website www.grin.com is an ideal platform for presenting term papers, final papers, scientific essays, dissertations and specialist books.

Visit us on the internet:

http://www.grin.com/

http://www.facebook.com/grincom

http://www.twitter.com/grin_com

INSTITUTE OF PRODUCTION & INVESTMENT RESEARCH

Industrial Management, Accounting and Corporate Planning

Georg-August University of Göttingen

Topic: **Potential and limits of Outsourcing Procurement**
With practical examples: E-Procurement at BMW Group
and Daimler Chrysler AG

Termpaper: Strategic and Operative Management in Manufacturing
Companies, 4 Credit points for the MBA-Examination
(Diplom) at the University of Göttingen

2nd Edition: December 2012 (English Edition)
translated from original German 1st Edition; 2004

Author:................. Martin Ruppe

I

II. Table of Abbreviations

B2B.....................Business-to-Business

BME...................Bundesverband Materialwirtschaft, Einkauf und Logistik e.V.

BMW...................Bayrische Motorenwerke

BPO....................Business Process Outsourcing

Cf. ....compare

CIO.....................Chief Information Officer

Diss.....................Dissertation

DPS.....................Desktop-Purchasing-System

Ed........................Editioner

EDP.....................Electronic Data Processing

EPS.....................Electronic Procurement Service

EPSP...................Electronic Procurement Service Provider

Et seq...................following page

ff........................following pages

fig. ....figure, illustration

HP.......................Hewlett-Packard

ICT.....................Information and communication technology

MCC...................Micro Compact Car

MRO...................Maintenance, Repair, Operation

PS.......................Procurement Services

PSP......................Procurement Service Provider

Resp....................Respectively

ROI.....................Return of Investment

Tab.......................Table

vol. ....Volume

ZfB......................Zeitschrift für Betriebswirtschaft

III.   Index of Tables

1. Introduction

The increasing complexity of the business environment and the internationalization of business activities in the past decades have led to an increase of market dynamics. For companies, it is therefore increasingly important to be flexible from the tactical and strategical point of view, to keep costs under control and to maintain or even increase their level of performance with regard to worldwide competition.[1]

Companies have to adjust their internal organizational structure concerning cost –and efficiency aspects, also with regard to the core competences each company specializes in. The outsourcing of competences to certain suppliers and service providers is regarded as a main strategy to secure competitiveness.[2]
Therefore, the usage of new communication -and IT-tools is getting more and more important.[3]

This paper shows the potential and limits of outsourcing the Procurement when companies try to restructure their organization. Beside conventional possibilities of outsourcing, new electronic procurement-solutions have become more popular during the last decades. The focus of this paper lies on such new electronic procurement-solutions. Chapter 2 describes the basics of Procurement and Outsourcing. Based on this, chapter 3 shows potential and limits of both, conventional solutions of outsourcing and also new modern solutions. To get a more practical view, the paper describes the topic by means of two examples from the automobile industry by BMW Group and the DaimlerChrysler AG. Finally, the paper gives a summary and a preview regarding upcoming business challenges of outsourcing procurement.

---

[1] cf. Koppelmann, (Outsourcing), p. 9.
[2] cf. Femerling, (Strategische Auslagerungsplanung), see foreword.
[3] cf.. Schneider, (Outsourcing), p. 7f.

1

2. Basics

2.1 Basics of Procurement

2.1.1 Definition and explanation of terms

The term *Procurement* is covering all company and market-related activities which help allocating necessary products a company cannot produce itself.[4]

In science and practise, the terms *Procurement* and *Purchasing/Buying* are partly used as synonyms.[5]

Thus, both terms are explained in the following section:

According to Arnold, in science the term "procurement" is almost always used as the process-related basic function before production and sales.[6] Dobler/Burt perceive procurement in a broader sense also including strategical functions: „The procurement process, or concept, encompasses a wider range of supply activities than those included in the purchasing function. And it typically includes a broadened view of the traditional buying role, with more buyer participation in related materials activities. [...] In comparison to the typical implementation of the purchasing concept, procurement essentially tends to be perceived in a broader and more proactive sense, with some focus on strategic matters.[7]

Purchasing is regarded as a subfunction of Procurement and rather concentrates on the buying-process of the productions factors.[8] Trading-firms consider Purchasing as a key-function. The tasks of the purchaser also cover responsibilities in sales. In industrial/ -manufacturing companies, purchasers are mainly responsible for market-related tasks, e.g. to negogiate buying real assets. Thus, the term *Purchasing* is perceived in a narrower sense.[9]

---

[4] Arnold, (Beschaffungsmanagement), p. 3.
[5] cf. Grochla/Schönbohm, (Beschaffung in der Unternehmung), p. 4f.
[6] Arnold, (Beschaffungsmanagement), p. 5.
[7] Dobler/Burt, (Purchasing and supply Management), p. 35f.
[8] cf. Corsten, (Lexikon der Betriebswirtschaftslehre), p. 108.
[9] cf. Grochla/Schönbohm, (Beschaffung), p.5f.

2.1.2 Functions and Responsibilities of Procurement

The main function of Procurement is the realization of customer's preferences on the procurement market.[10] Procurement functions can be structurized in different ways. Roland derives the single tasks in procurement- from the purchasing functions.[11]

The following section describes different views of procurement functions .

The varied use of the term procurement in theory and literature has its origin in the different functions attributed to it. Arnold, Heege and Tussing perceive the procurement functions in a narrower sense than the task of buying operation materials from the market. In a wider context, the allocation of manufacturing, human ressources and capital is also comprised in the term.[12] In a narrower sense Bloech and Rottenbacher consider only purchasing as a function of procurement.[13] In a broader context they also mention material planning as a procurement function.[14]

The functions of procurement are shown from a process-orientated point of view in table 1, structured into the different phases of procurement: Procurement preparation, initiation, completion, realisation and control.[15]

1. Procurement Preparation	• Identification of the procurement demand • Specification of the procurement demand
2. Procurement Initiation	• Supplier search –and selection • Soliciting offers and offer-analysis
3. Procurement completion	• Contract negotiation and completion • Order
4. Procurement realisation	• Supervision of the timely fullfilment of a contract • Control to keep always best logistical solution • Goods receipt and storage
5. Procurement control	• Supervision of goods receipt • Quality control • Supplier evaluation and invoice verification

Tab. 1 Functions of Procurement (process-oriented)[16]

---

[10] cf. Bichler, (Beschaffungs- und Lagerwirtschaft), p. 31.

[11] cf. Roland, (Beschaffungsstrategien), p. 12.

[12] cf. Arnolds/Heege/Tussing, (Materialwirtschaft und Einkauf), p. 20.

[13] cf. Bloech/Rottenbacher, (Materialwirtschaft), p. 9.

[14] ibid., p. 4.

[15] cf. Friedl, (Grundlagen) p. 64; Lippmann, (Beschaffungsmarketing), p. 50ff; Hammann/Lohrberg, (Beschaffungsmarketing), p. 7; Bichler, (Beschaffungs- und Lagerwirtschaft), p. 32.

[16] Source: own creation based on Roland, (Beschaffungsstrategien), p. 12f; Bichler, (Beschaffungs- und Lagerwirtschaft), p. 32.

During the first phase (Procurement preparation), the demand must be identified; followed by the search for suppliers and their selection. After a number of offers have been solicited and assessed, the contract negotiations can be finalized with an order. The fourth phase (Procurement realisation) is characterized by supervising the timeline of the contract and the best logistical solution. The last phase (Procurement control) consists of goods, supplier, invoice verification and quality control.

This kind of traditional procurement process as shown in table 1 can be organized even more efficiently by outsourcing certain phases to external service providers by using electronic procurement-solutions (E-Procurement). This will be focused on in chapter 3.

2.1.3 Objectives of Procurement

In general, a procurement target is regarded as the desired condition, resulting from actions within the field of procurement.[17]

The targets of procurement depend on business objectives and must be derived consequently from the corporate target system and must be coordinated with other departments' targets.[18]

The planning of the objectives of procurement is characterized by choosing one dominant objective. Afterwards secondary targets being compatible with the mainobjective can be defined. Then, it must be verified that the defined objectives of procurement are compatible with other departments' targets.[19]

The formal objectives (cost reduction, performance enhancing, maintaining autonomy) can be defined on the basis of the main objective of procurement (securing the supply of the company).[20]

In order to be able to determine concrete activities, the main objectives must be subdivided into global objectives and into more differentiated subordinateobjectives. [...] Friedl divides procurement objectives into strategic and tactical-operative targets according to their maturity.[21]

Strategical procurement targets are the securing of material supply, quality aspects, position on the procurement market and price stability. Friedl considers the

---

[17] cf. Friedl, (Grundlagen), p. 83f.
[18] cf. Hammann/Lohrberg, (Beschaffungsmarketing), p. 47.
[19] cf. Stangl, (Beschaffungsmarkforschung), p. 13.
[20] cf. Grochla/Schönbohm, (Beschaffung), p. 25ff.
[21] Friedl, (Grundlagen), p.103.

optimization of procurement costs, the securing of material quality, liquidity and the readiness to supply as tactical-operative targets, The concrete activities must then be allocated according to their respective maturity.[22] *Table 2* will give you a well-structured overview.

Strategical Objectives	Tactical-operative Objectives
1. Securing the material supply	**1. Securing the material supply**
• Mainting flexibility	• Regarding the purchase prices
• Mainting independency	• Regarding the administrative cost of Procurement
• Balance of portfolio	
• Securing the long-term growth rate	
• Diversification	**2. Securing the material quality**
2. Securing the quality	**3. Securing the liquidity**
• regarding the material	
• regarding the technological standard of the material	**4. Securing the readiness to supply**
• regarding the staff	
3. Securing the Procurement market position	
• Securing the buyer power	
• Maintaining the reputation of the company	
4. Securing the price stability	

Tab. 2: Objectives of Procurement[23]

[22] ibid., p.103.
[23] Source: own creation based on Friedl, (Grundlagen), p. 103.

2.2 Basics of Outsourcing

2.2.1 Definition and explanation of terms

Outsourcing is an artificial word, which derives from the Anglo-Saxon language on the basis of the words *outside, resource* and *using*. At the beginning of the 1990ies, the term *outsourcing* has been adopted by the experts on the German market in the course of congresses regarding Outsourcing.[24]

Outsourcing means that external sources are used for the supply of the company. Thus, the usage of external sources is based on purchase decisions.[25]

Furthermore, the term implicates, that ressources are handed over to third parties. Third parties can be e.g. a subsidiary, a service provider, a venture capital company or a third person completely unknown to the company. The first two options mentioned are often described as internal outsourcing, the last option as external outsourcing.[26]

The partially synonymous use of the terms *Outsourcing* and *Make-or-Buy* points to the same central point of both concepts, namely the question, if inhouse production should be outsourced to an external market partner or if it should be continued on their own premises. Classical make-or-buy-decisions are primarily used to cover peaks of demand by working together with an external partner. Outsourcing-decisions have are rather of strategical importance which result into a long-term cooperation with suppliers.[27]

The fifties were marked by changes in the big companies. Several departments and auxilliary plants were increasingly outsourced to service providers orcommitted to third parties respectively (Outsourcing of complete functions) in order to reduce costs.[28]

Since the end of the eighties, the motivation for outsourcing was increased by the economical pressure resulting from internationalisation and rising market dynamics.

---

[24] cf. Horchler, (Outsourcing), p. 3.
[25] cf. Koppelmann, (Outsourcing), p. 2.
[26] cf. Köhler-Frost/Baaken, (Outsourcing – Eine strategische Allianz besonderen Typs), p. 13.
[27] Reichmann/Palloks, (Make-or-Buy-Kalkulationen im modernen Beschaffungsmangement), in: Hahn/Kaufmann, (Handbuch Industrielles Beschaffungsmanagement), p. 419-421.
[28] cf. Koppelmann, (Outsourcing), p. 13f.

Changes in cost and organizational structures were necessary for the maintaining of stability and flexibility of the companies.[29]

Since the beginning of the nineties, traditional structures have been changed and new organisational concepts were launched; e.g. new management concepts like Lean Management /-Production.[30] The Lean-concept forms the basis of outsourcing.[31] It is based on concepts for the internal organisation of a company and on concepts for the external relationships between companies.[32]

Internal Lean concepts are e.g. Just-in-time[33], Kaizen[34] and the fractal organisation[35]. Outsourcing as well as Single –or Doublesourcing[36] and Globalsourcing[37] are concepts for external relationships. The opposite pole to Outsourcing is Insourcing. If the productivity of the staff within a company is increasing, but at the same time the sales volume is already at maximum level, the company will be searching internally for new employment (Insourcing) in order to avoid high social costs.[38]

2.2.2 Fields of Outsourcing

Basically, Outsourcing is possible in all areas of a company. Attempting to structure fields of Outsourcing means having a closer look at the organizational structure of a company. Koppelmann structures the different managment-levels of the company by differentiating between the first, second and third managment-level.[39]

The first management-level is represented by the top managament/ executive management, whereas Outsourcing in this context covers typical management staff functions. This concerns the consulting of the executive management. In the future,

---

[29] cf. Warnecke, (Die Fraktale Fabrik – Revolution der Unternehmenskultur), p. 12ff.
[30] cf. Weber, (Alternative Organisationskonzepte der betrieblichen Datenverarbeitung), p. 6-38.
[31] cf. Womack/Jones/Roos, (Die zweite Revolution in der Autoindustrie), p. 77ff.
[32] ibid., p. 77ff.
[33] Just-in-Time decribes the organisational principle of internal and external supplier systems regarding system components needed for the production. cf. Womack/Jones/Roos, (ibid.), p. 67ff.
[34] Kaizen describes the collective process towards a continuously stepwise improvment of the production process. cf. Ibid, p. 61ff.
[35] The fractal organisation is self-organised ist selbstorgansierend and high dynamically. It consists out of flexible teams which solve tasks and problems independently and on own response. cf. Warnecke, (Die Fraktale Fabrik – Revolution der Unternehmenskultur), p. 136ff.
[36] These concepts describe activities concerning a reduction to limit the number of suppliers donw to only one or two. cf. Bichler, (Beschaffungs- und Lagerwirtschaft), p. 42-43.
[37] Globalsourcing is seen as a systematical extension of the procurement policy towards internaional procurement sources with strategical character. ibid, p. 43.
[38] Koppelmann, (Outsourcing), p. 2.
[39] cf. ebenda, p.7f.

company-owned consulting-staff functions within big organisations will be outsourced completely or at least outsourced in relation to different projects.[40]

At the second managment-level, the course is set concerning the organisational functions.[41] It depends on the organizational strcuture of a company which functions (Procurement, Sales, Controlling, HR, R&D) will be addressed with regard to Outsourcing, however,as it is not possible to cover all functions at the same time, it must be decided which function should be adressed to what extent. Especially in the field of Procurement it is not only possible to bundle C-products to get A-products, but it is also possible to optimize processes in order to reduce fixed costs.[42]

The possibility to outsource several tasks leads to a tremendous rise of outsourcing activities at the third managment level. With regard to Procurement, e.g. the entire market research regarding procurement can be outsourced.[43]

The Outsourcing complete company-functions as for example the market research regarding procurement to external service providers is also called "Business Process Outsourcing (BPO).

2.2.3 Objectives of Outsourcing

By thoroughly planning the outsourcing of internal services or rather of complete company functions, the concentration on the actual core competencies of the company will be possible again. By engaging certain ancillary services, companies can profit from cheaper supplier cost-structures and can thususe this cost advantage to increase their revenue.[44]

In order to strenghten the market position competencies must comply with the defined targets which means thatcertain tasks can be outsourced with overall better conditions for the company. At the same time a possible loss of competence must be avoided to maintain a stable competitive position.[45]

Quinn states that „Core-competency-with-outsourcing strategies make special sense in rapidly changing marketplaces and technological situations. They decrease risks,

---

[40] cf. Koppelmann, (Outsourcing), p. 8.
[41] cf. Schanz, (Organisationsgestaltung), p. 113ff.
[42] Koppelmann, (Outsourcing), p. 8.
[43] cf. Koppelmann, (Outsourcing), p. 9.
[44] Reichmann/Palloks, (Make-or-Buy-Kalkulationen im modernen Beschaffungsmanagement), p. 421.
[45] Koppelmann, (Outsourcing), p. 3.

shorten cycle times, lower investments, flatten and lean organizations, and make their sponsors more responsive to customer needs".[46]

Based on the reasons for outsourcing procurement functions described in chapter 2.2.1 (e.g. increasing economical pressure caused by the internationlisation and dynamisation of the markets) three objectives of outsourcing can be derived: *Cost, Output,* and *Flexibility*.[47]

The aim of the cost objective is lowering the costs. In order to reach this objective in terms of Output, different suppliers on the market must be evaluated. Suppliers, which follow the economical principle and offer better input, transformation, or output solutions, should be chosen.

So far companies concentrated on lean factor combinations without idle capacities (cost optimized capacities and active pricing) to achieve the desired flexibility objectives. The aim is to balance the fluctuations of the procurement quantities of the outsourcing company.[48]

What are the chances resp. the possibilities to outsource procurement and how can the above-mentioned objectives be achieved? This will be explained in the next chapter.

---

[46] Hahn/Kaufmann, (Handbuch), p. 45.
[47] ibid., p. 4f.
[48] ibid., p. 4f.

3. Potential and limits of Outsourcing Procurement

3.1 Potential of Outsourcing Procurement

As explained in chapter 2, the market forces companies to be structuredmore effectively and to work more efficiently. With regard to Procurement, it means to bundle all the power and concentrate on core activities; and in case of need trying to outsource this branch at a low cost. In order to achieve these objectives, a strategic concept with regard to the company activities will be necessary.

The following section presents an overview of conventional and modern electronic possibilties to outsource procurement.

3.1.1 Conventional Possibilities

The increasing shifting of activities to external service providers requires a new positioning of procurement by establishing an even better cooperative collaboration with efficient suppliers.[49] This leads to the outsourcing of complete company functions, e.g. of procurement (Business Process Outsourcing – BPO), whereas in general strategic objectives are being pursued.[50]

Conventional Procurement Services (PS) supply the company with the necessary cost-effective and /or high-value external products or services and PS enable the company to concentrate on its core business. A certain technical standard is thePrerequisite for this supply. PS are characterized by a low service and technical level.[51]

Typical examples for Procurement Services (PS) are *Price- or Sourcing agencies,* which have the task to identify a supplier ideally corresponding to the criteria given by the company, whereas the cost is one of the most important criteria in this aspect. Price agencies mainly work in the field of investment goods and mostly for high-value one-time demands.

---

[49] Reichmann/Palloks, (Make-or-Buy-Kalkulationen im modernen Beschaffungsmanagement), p. 420.
[50] Pulic (2003): Aktuelle Trends in der Beschaffung indirekter Materialen, Online in the Internet:
http://www.procurementletter.de/archiv/2003/pL-122003.pdf
(Status 11.12.2003; call-off 28.05.2004)
[51] cf. Tripp, (E-Procurement Services), p. 296f.

As a further possibility, *Trade-Service-Provider* beside their normal trade-function also offer to take over certain procurementprocesses, e.g. the identification of procurement demand with regard to customers stocks or the automatical re-filling of the stock. But their main tasks are taking over the stockholding-function, simplifying warehouse-logistics and reducing costs on the part of the customer. The procuring of special goods from far away, e.g. from South-East-Asia or from South-America, could be outsourced to Drop Shipping-Service-Providers.[52]

In order to achieve the cost target (cf. Section 2.2.3), an external service provider could be commissioned by which cost degression effects could be reached by using the advantages of specialising. Thus, the company could outsource the procurement of C-products. The service provider bundles C-products to A-products. The fixed costs in procurement-are reduced with the parallel rising of quantities, while the cost structure will be more transparent. An attached table (*appendix A 01*) describes the ratio of order-value and purchasing volume of A, B and Cproducts. It shows the low value of C-products and its high demand, whereas A and B products are of high value but are in low demand.[53]

Further possibilities to increase the *Output* by outsourcing are e.g. the usage of more efficient transformation technologies and the usage of special know-how of other providers. The Output of the service-provider represents the Input of Outsourcing companies. By the conclusion of contracts new business relationships are possible which can reduce investment risks of the outsourcing company. Better output solutions can be achieved by a faster and more reliable delivery of the service providers.[54]

The reliability of the supplier must at least correspond to one's own reliability. The flexibility of procurement is very important in this aspect, as different suppliers and their different capacities canbe used to their best effect.[55]

A high *Flexibility* of the outsourcing company can be achieved by a suitable sales policy.[56] "By establishing a supplier warehouse for the manufacturer the lead time can be optimized and thus the the stock can be reduced. The supplier manages the re-

---

[52] cf. Schneider (Outsourcing von Beschaffungsdienstleistungen), p. 9-22.
[53] cf. Arnolds/Heege/Tussing, (Materialwirtschaft und Einkauf), p. 39ff.
[54] cf. Koppelmann, (Outsourcing), p. 4f.
[55] Femerling, (Strategische Auslagerungsplanung), p. 7.
[56] cf. Koppelmann, (Outsourcing), p. 4f.

filling-process of the stock according to the net requirements planning of the manufacturer."[57]

Thus, it is possible to compensate fluctuating procurement quantities of the outsourcing company, whereas a self-dependent service provider works more efficiently and cheaper than the outsourcing company.[58] At the same time, capacity and amortisation risks are reduced by outsourcing. Especially in case of an insecure, unstable, small and/ or time-limited procurement demand the consulting of service providers can be very important. Thus, the strategy of outsourcing becomes an important instrument with regard to the risk policy of a company.[59] Mutual trust between business partners is a crucial factor and the basis for any cooperation in order to achieve the procurement objectives. On the one hand, trust is the confidence to being able to meet the expectations of the business partner, and on the other hand, to also being able to predict business behaviour.[60]

The increasing integration of internet technology into business processes is another option for outsourcing. More and more companies realize that they have to adapt their procurement organisation to the digital age due to increasing market dynamics,[61] thus creating a new dimension iof procurement, reducing interpersonal contacts and focussing at the same time on the actual procurement process. In the procurement departments, the transformation from manual filling out of paper forms to digital business processing is taking place.[62]

The transition from Conventional Procurement Service Providers (PSP) to Electronic Procurement Service Providers (EPSP) is rather smooth and depends on computerized support. A PSP can develop by itself into an EPSP by increasing the digital part, e.g. the usage of an internet-based technology.[63]

E-Procurement and E-Procurement Service Providers (EPSP) become more and more important. Thus, the following chapter gives an overview regarding E-Procurement and describes different types of E-Procurement Service Provider.

---

[57] Reichmann/Palloks, (Make-or-Buy-Kalkulationen im modernen Beschaffungsmanagement), p. 421.
[58] cf. Koppelmann, (Outsourcing), p. 4f.
[59] Femerling, (Strategische Auslagerungsplanung), p. 7.
[60] cf. Dyer/Chu, (The determinants of trust in supplier-automaker relationships in the US, Japan and Korea), p. 260.
[61] cf. Buchholz/Bach, (The Evolution of Netsourcing business models), p. 5.
[62] cf. Hartmann, (Successful Indroduction of B2B Electronic Marketplace Projects), p. 12f.
[63] Tripp, (E-Procurement Services), p. 296.

E-Procurement is the electronic realization of procurement processes, covering internal –and/ or external market related activities, which are mainly based on Information and Communication Technology (ICT) and are focussed on providing the products a company cannot produce itself.[64] This can be internal approval processes preceding the actual placing of a procurement order. In case of market-related activities the company will contactexternal partners like suppliers. E-Procurement can be used in the operative and in the strategical procurement. The goal is to reduce process costs and product prices by accelerating procurement processes.[65]

Process costs, especially labour costs as the biggest cost factor, can be reduced by automatic handling. According to a survey, the reduction of process costs by means of E-Procurement is regarded as a crucial strategical objective by 85% of the polled companies.[66] Thus, error frequency and related costs for correction of the entire procurement process can be reduced.

Service companies, offering electronic procurement solutions are called *System providers*. They offer procurement process solutions for customers, who would have to use expensive standard software packages for their small procurement demands. System providers have the task to develop standard interfaces, replacing the manual input of procurement processes into the customers cost accounting modules; thus, helping to reduce labour costs.

The goal is to shorten and to accelerate processes. *Full-Service-Providers* pursue the same goal. Full-Service-Providers additionally offer Procurement-Marketing Systems and Management-Information Systems, whereas they invest into high-capacity IT-systems, into the development of business relationships and into powerful databases.[67]

Purchasing-Card-Service Providers help to outsource certain parts of the procurement process, as for example the gathering of procurement demands data, control of access authorisation or accounting control, thus, procurement processes

---

[64] Bogaschewsky, (Elektronischer Einkauf), p. 13.
[65] cf. Tripp, (E-Procurement Services), p. 294.
[66] Pulic, (2003): Aktuelle Trends in der Beschaffung indirekter Materialen, Online in the Internet:
  http://www.procurementletter.de/archiv/2003/pL-122003.pdf
  (Status 11.12.2003; call-off 28.05.2004)
[67] cf. Schneider, (Outsourcing von Beschaffungsdienstleistungen), p. 19.

can be organized more efficiently. Purchasing-Card-Service Providers are for example big banks or credit card companies. Purchasing Cards are a special type of credit cards and depend on the acceptance of the suppliers.[68] The main difference to a conventional credit card is that the company, where the card holder is employed, receives the transaction data from the Purchsasing-Card-Service Provider, and has thus control over the use of the card. The physical handling of paper documents, e.g. orders or invoices is replaced by electronic transactions, which allows the company to cut process costs. This service can also support the company's Management Information System.[69] An important factor for running a succesful E-Procurement is not only intelligent use of IT-technology but also the strategically and technically profound integration[70] of the instruments of E-Procurement into existing organisational structures.[71] E-Procurement-Instruments are newly developed internet-based applications, for example *electronic markets* (portals, electronic marketplaces, purchase channels) and *Desktop-Purchasing-Systems*. Portals are for example search engines. They are different compared to electronic marketplaces and purchase channels, because on the one hand they do generate a lot of attention, but on the other side they only provide information and do not support transactions.[72]

Electronic marketplaces are virtual places, where supply meets demand.

The Internet enables suppliers from all over the world to enter into business, thusincreasing even more the national competitive pressure. Commercial options are for example auctions (e.g. "ebay").

Electronic purchasing channels have the task to support the procurement process electronically, wheras they control the access authorization of the buyers and the compliance with the company's Procurement Policy.[73]

Desktop-Purchasing-Systems (DSP) are software applications based on internet technology supporting electronically internal and external procurement processes. The core of DPS is a product catalog which employees can access via their

---

[68] cf. Schneider, (Outsourcing von Beschaffungsdienstleistungen), p. 23.

[69] cf. iMPOWER (2003): Purchasing Cards, Online in the Internet:
http://www.nepp.org.uk/80256d8900466fd6/httppublicassets/79c0e77ea7997e4380256db20046cd6e/$file/technical+overview+-+purchasing+cards.pdf
(Status 10.01.2003; call-off 08.06.2004)

[70] cf. Buchholz/Bach, (The Evolution of Netsourcing business models), p. 5.

[71] Kaup, wallmedien AG (2003): eProcurement-Systeme im Einsatz, Online in the Internet:
http://www.ecin.de/strategie/healthcare/print.html (Status 31.07.2003; call-off 11.05.2004)

[72] cf. Kersten, (Geschäftsmodelle und Perspektiven des industriellen Einkaufs im Electronic Business), p. 21-37.

[73] cf. Schneider/Schnetkamp, (E-Markets), p.98.

computer.[74] As a result of investing into this technology, companies can reduce product prices. Thus, a higher transparency can be created and better conditions can be negogiated. Furthermore, this leads to an acceleration of the procurement process as informations is transported faster and more precisely. Thus, significant delays can be avoided.[75]

Chapter 3.1.3 will give an example within the automobile industry which describes the process of outsourcing certain parts of procurement with the help of E-Procurement.

Employing E-Procurement Service Providers (EPSP) instead of conventional service providers has many advantages.

Electronic Service Providers support the outsourcing company based on electronic procurement processes. This is the main differences between these two types of providers, wheras EPS mainly use Information and Communication Technology (ICT), e.g. the Internet. Additional interface costs incurring when additional service provider are used can be eliminated by reverting to EPSP. When companies plan to expand on an international level, they are often faced with the problem of setting up quickly and smoothly the new Sales –and Production organisation. In this aspect, EPSP offer further additional benefits. The supplier structure within the new target country is often unknown to the nationally established procurement department. In this context EPSP can help to establish quickly an international supply and thus a faster international expansion of the company.[76] Not only certain parts of the procurement can be outsourced, but it is also possible to outsource the entire procurement process to an E-Procurement Servive Provider. Neither resources nor Know-How must be provided from the company to the EPSP, thus the company can focus on its strategically relevant core business.[77]

According to a survey among leading German companies[78], more than 50% of companies interested in outsourcing expect an improvement with regard to costs and

---

[74] cf. Dolmetsch, R. (eProcurement: Sparpotential im Einkauf), p. 152.
[75] cf. Walser/Zimmer, (E-procurement), p. 11ff. or: ibid (1999): Online in the Internet: http://www.pwcglobal.com/de/ger/ins-sol/publ/ger_510_089_05.pdf (Status 1999; call-off 27.05.2004)
[76] Tripp, (E-Procurement Services), p. 299.
[77] Hohaus, (Zehn vor zwölf für den Einkauf), p. 8ff.
[78] Survey of BME, of Siemens AG and the European School of Business in Reutlingen, (Aktuelle Trends bei der Beschaffung indirekter Materialen), Status: August / September 2003, number of participants: 1.052 chief buyers / strategical procurement managers of leading German companies across all branches

to purchasing information and a successful containment of Maverick Buying by E-Procurement[79]. Dr. H. Hildebrandt, the Managing Director of BME (Bundesverband Materialwirtschaft, Einkauf und Logistik e.V.), comments on the survey: „The survey shows that the majority of companies see Business Process Outsourcing (BPO) in relation with E-Procurement as the main backup for the achievement of strategic procurement objectives."[80] These objectives are not realized by only one service provider, but particularly as a result of professional planning and re-organsiation. In procurement, triggered by the automobile industry, there have been many initiatives regarding the reorganization of the manufacturer-supplier-relationship. Thus, more manufacturers now benefit from the advantages of a regional supplier, which are supply one manufacturer to a 100%. With regard to high-quality products the business trend goes towards Single Sourcing, which can be seen as a traditional procurement strategy. Single Sourcing means that all demands of the company areordered by a central procurement department from one external supplier. The aims of Single Sourcing are to combine buyer power, to secure a standard communication channel, to avoid Maverick Buying and to guarantee an invulnerable process regarding commercial and legal aspects.[81]

3.1.3 Outsourcing with E-Procurement using the example of BMW Group

In the automobile industry, a relatively high percentage (65%) of added value is being outsourced to external service providers. In the 2015 even 75% will supposedly be realized by external suppliers.[82] The term *added value* will be used many times in the following section. Its calculation will be explained in detail in *appendix 03*.

Automobile manufactures rather concentrate on product development and on the strengthening of the car brand, while procurement, production and logistics are

---

[79] Maverick Buying describes the „wild" procurement of goods from suppliers without negotiated contracts and without informing the strategical procurement managment about these activities. Maverick Buying blockst he possibilites of the company to utilise their market potential and to practice an efficient supplier managment
[80] ECIN, (2003): Beschaffung: eProcurement und Outsourcing gehen Hand in Hand, Online in the Internet: http://www.ecin.de/news/2003/11/04/06390/ (Status 31.07.2003; call-off 11.05.2004)
[81] Reichmann/Palloks, (Make-or-Buy-Kalkulationen im modernen Beschaffungsmanagement), p. 420.
[82] University Kitzbühel, (2003): New challenges in the Automotive Industry, in: Laforsch, M., Mielke, BearingPoint GmbH (2003): Das Outsourcing Momentum nutzen, Online in the Internet: http://www.logistik-inside.de/sixcms4/sixcms_upload/media/1073/laforsch_neu1.pdf), (Status 01.07.2003; call-off 05.06.2004)

outsourced.[83] Carmakers focus on the brand experience and on the individuality of the brand, thus these departments are never outsourced. Brand components e.g. motors for windscreen wipers or seat components which are invisible to customers, can be   outsourced without cannibalisation effects and thus contribute to the reduction of costs and of the risk.[84]

By chosing the E-Procurement Solution *ARIBA,* the *BMW Group* has decided to outsource a part of their procurement to the Internet.[85] The EPSP *ARIBA* offers different procurement solutions for companies, e.g. strategic consultancy, business analysis or interface solutions for manufactures and suppliers.[86] ARIBA works as a system provider for BMW taking over the procurement preperation and initiation (please cf. Tab. 01). The basis of E-Procurement is a Multi-Supplier-Catalogue, which comprises the offers of all different suppliers. The catalogue is also administrated by ARIBA. But the purchasers of BMW get to decide themselves which products will be added to the catalogue at what price. This also depends on the negotiations with the partners of BMW.   These products are MRO-products (Maintenance, Repair, Operation), e.g. spare parts, toolings, office equipment. These are all products which are not directly linked to the production. The suppliers send their product data to ARIBA. Afterwards the service provider prepares the data for BMW.[87] These factors are very beneficial for the BMW Group asprocesses are tighter and more efficient.[88]

BMW expects a quick Return on Investment (ROI), because the Investment in the low double-digit million euro sum will already break even after one year. 90,000 employees will use the Desktop-Purchasing-System as the new procurement

---

[83] Laforsch/Mielke, BearingPoint GmbH (2003): Das Outsourcing Momentum nutzen, Online in the Internet: http://www.logistik-inside.de/sixcms4/sixcms_upload/media/1073/laforsch_neu1.pdf), (Status 01.07.2003; call-off 05.06.2004)

[84] Chapman/Mielke/Stratil, (Cross-Brand Collaboration in the Automotive Industry), in Laforsch/Mielke, BearingPoint GmbH (2003): Das Outsourcing Momentum nutzen, Online in the Internet: http://www.logistik-inside.de/sixcms4/sixcms_upload/media/1073/laforsch_neu1.pdf), (Status 01.07.2003; call-off 05.06.2004)

[85] cf. InformationWeek (2000): E-Procurement – BMW geht eigene Wege, Online in the Internet: http://www.informationweek.de/index.php3?/channels/channel08/001440b.htm, (Status 02.06.2000; call-off 05.06.2004)

[86] cf. ARIBA Inc. (2004): Solutions Overview, Online in the Internet: http://www.ariba.com/solutions/solutions_overview.cfm, (Status 05.06.2004; call-off 05.06.2004)

[87] cf. InformationWeek (2000): E-Procurement – BMW geht eigene Wege, Online in the Internet: http://www.informationweek.de/index.php3?/channels/channel08/001440b.htm, (Status 02.06.2000; call-off 05.06.2004)

[88] cf. BMW Group (2003): Business report 2000: Produktion und Beschaffung, Online in the Internet: http://www.bmwgroup.com/d/nav/index.html?http://www.bmwgroup.com/d/0_0_www_bmwgroup_com/2_investor_relations/2_2_publikationen/2_2_1_geschaeftsbericht_00/2_2_1_3_inalt_gb_0/0/2_2_1_3_3_konzern/2_2_1_3_3_5_produktion.shtml, (Status 28.09.2003; call-off 05.06.2004)

solution. Furthermore, several process steps will not be needed any more and transcription errors will be eliminated, asthe process time of an order will be reduced from 65 minutes to 17 minutes, which will lead toa reduction of process costs. In the automobile industry, the average order-process-time is 100 minutes. By using the electronic process, BMW hopes for further price advantages.[89]

3.2 Limits of Outsourcing Procurement

Today, Outsourcing is often regarded as a kind of magical weapon or as a universal remedy in economically difficult situations.[90] Outsourcing of core competences, e.g. outsourcing the procurement to an external service provider doess not only have advantages, but also bears risks and limits as in contrast to support processes, core competences contribute directly to the company's added value.[91] The decision for Outsourcing has a rather strategic character and usually leads to a long-term business relationship with external partners.[92] Outsourcing the procurement can only be realized to a certain extent, as inspite of many advantages reducing the vertical range of manufacture also bears many risks.[93] Resulting problems are the loss of Know-How, less possibilities to control the processes as well as as synergy problems between external supply and internal production.[94]

3.2.1 The problem of Know-How-loss

Outsourcing is a big decision with major consequences for a company.. The company must be aware of the fact that some of the employees in procurement will have to leave the company. Thus, when considered in the medium term, the decision for outsourcing cannot be easily reversed. The loss of human capital resp. the loss of employees is synonymous with a Know-How-loss for the company. Especially in

---

[89] cf. InformationWeek (2000): E-Procurement – BMW geht eigene Wege, Online in the Internet:
  http://www.informationweek.de/index.php3?/channels/channel08/001440b.htm,
  (Status 02.06.2000; call-off 05.06.2004)
[90] cf. Koppelmann, (Outsourcing), p. 6.
[91] Meinhold/Grobla, Siemens AG (2004): Outtasking schafft neue Handlungsspielräume, Online in
  the Internet: http://www.ecin.de/strategie/outtasking/print.html
  (Status 13.05.2004; call-off 19.05.2004)
[92] cf. Köhler-Frost, (Outsourcing – Eine strategische Allianz besonderen Typs), p. 27.
[93] Pointner, (Umbruch in der Automobilindustrie – Von den Grenzen des Outsourcing), p. 151.
[94] cf. Koppelmann, (Outsourcing), p. 6f.

case of the failing of an outsourcing relationship, high financial investments for the recreation of lost Know-How will be the consequence.[95]

The manufacturer *MCC smart GmbH* has already reached the limits of outsourcing. With a complete new project, Mercedes-Benz relies on the knowledge pool of specialised suppliers and wants to exploit the advantages of outsourcing to the extremes, by trying to reach a real net output ratio of only 5%.[96] With a current vertical penetration of 8%, Mercedes-Benz has almost reached the limits with *smart* as a „field of learning". To further reduce the vertical penetration at this point now seems critical, because the entire Car-Know-How could be lost. Nevertheless, a vertical penetration of 0% seemspossible, provided that there is a strong competition among the automotive suppliersso that in case of the abrupt ending of an outsourcing relationship, suppliers can be replaced and costs are still under control. Additionally, strong networking competences will be necessary forthe brand integrators.[97]

3.2.2 Loss of control

The more company divisons are outsourced, the more complex the monitoring of the contractually stipulated work will be.[98] Due to the increasingnumber of interfaces, it will become harder to maintain a direct coordination. Thus, increased demands on s and new ways of communication will be necessary. Especially, if companies go for a zero-error-concept, a constant exchange of information should be granted.[99]

Exchange of information with the outsourcing service provider for example per email is often not sufficient and must be supported by weekly or monthly personal contacts between both business partners which requires a certain flexibility of the company at the same time . Furthermore, the pricing of the procurement materials is a problem, as it is not easy to calculate, and can thus ilead to relationship problems among the business partners. In the medium term, the company will be virtually at the outsourcing provider's mercy, even if the initial prices are favorable. Thus, potential future rises in prices should be contractually stipulated beforehand.[100]

---

[95] cf. Köhler-Frost, (Outsourcing – Eine strategische Allianz besonderen Typs), p. 30.

[96] Pointner, (Umbruch in der Automobilindustrie),pS. 153.

[97] ibid., p. 263.

[98] Pointner, (Umbruch in der Automobilindustrie), p. 61.

[99] cf. Koppelmann, (Outsourcing), p. 7.

[100] cf. Köhler-Frost, (Outsourcing – Eine strategische Allianz besonderen Typs), p. 30.

On the one hand, the company will suffer from the increased efforts regarding the monitoring of the contractual obligations, but on the other hand, there are also advantages, as an internal efficiency control will be established. Furthermore, it is possible to claim the contract penalty when it comes to an insufficient performance of a contract, e.g. delivery delays caused by the outsourcing provider. Thus, the financial damage for the company will be limited and the costs for production downtime can be equalized.[101]

The radical step of outsourcing complete core competences to an external service provider has a lot of hidden traps, which are mostly underestimated by companies, because they give away their possibilities to control the business. In contrast to this radical outsourcing strategy, the Siemens AG refers to a classical version of outsourcing – the so-called *Outtasking*. Instead of outsourcing complete business processes, only subtasks are outsourced to the external service provider, e.g. the Procurement Initiation. The advantage for the company is reducing costs on the one hand, and creating scope for financial tasks and helps the company keeping control regarding certain infrastructures and decision-making processes.[102]

3.2.3 Reduction of Synergy

After having discussed the question which areas of procurement should be ousourced and which ones should be kept within the company, the importance of combining these two issues will be explained in the following.

Thus, a solution regarding common interfaces must be found. It has to be considered that the market success of a company depends on a constant implementation of innovative technologies with regard to products, procurement and production processes. An outsourcing company which is e.g. strongly connected by Single Sourcing to only one supplier has no influence any more on the speed of innovation, thus running the risk of not keeping up with the market.[103]

---

[101] ibid, p. 61.
[102] Meinhold/Grobla, Siemens AG (2004): Outtasking schafft neue Handlungsspielräume, Online in the Internet: http://www.ecin.de/strategie/outtasking/print.html
(Status 13.05.2004; call-off 19.05.2004)
[103] cf. Koppelmann, (Outsourcing), p. 7f.

3.2.4 Limits of Outsourcing Procurement with E-Procurment using the example of DaimlerChrysler AG

The *DaimlerChrysler AG* with its project "PC Global" will serve as an example. The company tried to outsource certain procurement-units by Desktop-Outsourcing to *Hewlett-Packard* (HP).[104] The procurement and the maintenance of all desktop-computers, notebooks and net-components should be completely outsourced to HP as a Full-Service-provider. The contract volume amounted to roughly half a billion Euro.[105]

The planning of demand was rather intransparent until then at DaimlerChrysler and a standard desktop quality management had been missing. The consequences were a high complexity, high costs for troubleshooting as well as a lacking flexibility. The decisive factor for the project was a funding gap, which occurred on a rotational basis every time a new system software was launched. The last time it occurred was in 2001, and the next time will be in 2005 when the next launch will take place. It was DaimlerChrysler's aim to roll-out the new applications in a simpler and faster way as well as creating standardized processes and standards for hardware and services. HP, as the solew supplier was supposed to receive a monthly lump-sum andhad the task to establish transparencyin order to reduce costs per unit and to reduce the expenses for hardware and services. In February 2003, the contract with HP was concluded and had a contract period of five years.It was planned to standardize from 130,000 up to 150,000 computer jobs at 153 factories in more than 10000 subsidiaries.[106]

The first problems occurred, when more than 3,000 special applications among which were very complex products for necessary engineering functions had to be administrated, packed and implemented on the computers of the DaimlerChysler employees by HP.[107] Already in November 2003, the carmaker negotiated with HP

---

[104] cf. Seeger, (2003): Desktop-Outsourcing bei DaimlerChrysler, Online in the Internet:
http://www.cio.de/index.cfm?PageID=300&cat=det&maid=2894&aid=3,
(Status 03.11.2003; call-off 07.06.2004)

[105] Manager-magazin.de (2003): Daimler-Projekt: Rückschlag für HP, Online in the Internet:
http://rs.net-hh.de/ebusiness/artikel/0,2828,275926,00.html,
(Status 28.11.2003; call-off 07.06.2004)

[106] cf. Seeger, (2003): Desktop-Outsourcing bei DaimlerChrysler, Online in the Internet:
http://www.cio.de/index.cfm?PageID=300&cat=det&maid=2894&aid=3,
(Status 03.11.2003; call-off 07.06.2004)

[107] cf. Seeger, (2003): Desktop-Outsourcing bei DaimlerChrysler, Online in the Internet:
http://www.cio.de/index.cfm?PageID=300&cat=det&maid=2894&aid=3,
(Status 03.11.2003; call-off 07.06.2004)

regarding the cancellation of the contract, as HP had already come to their limits during the pilot phase of the project "PC Global".[108] An interview of the weekly IT-magazine „Computerwoche" with Sue Unger (CIO – Chief Information Officer of DaimlerChrysler AG) confirmed, that even a big company like Hewlett Packard could reach its organisational limits with a project of such dimensions. An outsourcing project of such extents like „PC Gobal" cannot be outsourced to only one service provider. The reasons for the failure are mainly to be found in service as HP could not guarantee a constant world- wide high-quality service. Meanwhile, other procurement sources are used again as well, e.g. Siemens, IBM or Dell. Nevertheless, DaimlerChrysler maintains its goal to standardise hardware specifications, as thecarmaker was able to bundle the procurement demand successfully.[109]

4. Summary and Future Prospects

The aim of this paper was to present the potential and limits of outsourcing procurement. Conventional and new electronic procurement solutions (E-Procurement) were introduced on the basis of theoretical foundations of procurement and outsourcing. Especially, the potential and limits of procurement outsourcing were presented on the basis ofpractical examples from the automobile industry.

It was shown that companies are able to increase the efficiency of processes by outsourcing; especially via E-Procurement. The example of the BMW Group illustrates how some parts of the procurement can be outsourced successfully into the internet, whereas BMW used ARIBA as E-Procurement-Solution. . Furthermore, the risks and limits of outsourcing were described in the main part of the paper. The example of DaimlerChrysler AG shows, that the decision to outsource complete procurement processes has its organizational limits. Outsourcing procurement can lead to a know-how loss, a loss of control and to syngergy problems for the company.

---

[108] cf. Müller, CNET Networks Inc. (2003): HP verliert Outsourcing-Deal mit DaimlerChrysler, Online in the Internet: http://www.zdnet.de/news/business/0,39023142,39117851,00.htm, (Status 28.11.2003; call-off 08.06.2004)

[109] Sawall, Internet.com (2004): Daimler-Chrysler beerdigt Plan alle Desktop-PCs von nur einem Zulieferer zu beziehen, Online in the Internet: http://de.internet.com/index.php?id=2028738, (Status 28.05.2004; call-off 08.06.2004)

Companies are constantly confronted with cost pressure caused by globilization and other market influences. Thus, they must adopt their core business to the changing market conditions at frequent intervals. Thus, the demand for external service provider will increase in the future. The necessary flexibility can be achieved by outsourcing procurement processes or at least parts of it to external service provider.[110] The risk can be reduced by accurate planning, organisation and handling of the outsourcing process. Outsourcing must be integrated carefully into the organizational strategy and must be constantly adapted and developed in order to guarantee success.[111] The strategic character of a decision forcalls requires meticulous monitoring. Companies must reassess constantly if their flexibility can be maintained in the dynamic business environment and if efficiency can be further increased by outsourcing.

5. Appendix

A 01: Order value and Order quantity [112]

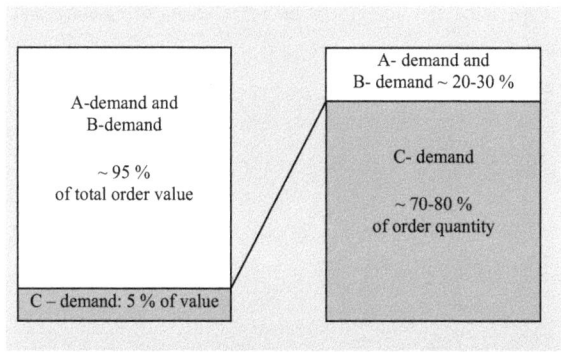

With the help of an ABC-Analysis, it is possible to classify goods, often intothree classes (A,- B,- und C-goods).[113]

---

[110] cf. Schneider, (Outsourcing von Beschaffungsdienstleistungen), p. 80.
[111] cf. Horchler, (Outsourcing), p. 254.
[112] Source: self-made according to cf. Schneider, (Outsourcing von Beschaffungsdienstleistungen), p. 10.
[113] cf. Arnolds/Heege/Tussing, (Materialwirtschaft und Einkauf), p. 39-41.

A 02: Calculation of vertical integration & explanation:

The *vertical integration* is a monetary assessment of a company's own - productivity/performance or output.[114]

The *added value* is the difference of total output (e.g. turnover, change in stock) and intermediate inputs (i.e. externally purchased material, external services, interest). [115]

The *proportion of added value* depends on the vertical integration:

$$\text{Proportion of added value in \%} = \frac{\text{vertical integration}}{\text{total output}}$$

Vertical integration and total output have the same quantity (monetary unit). By multiplying it by 100, the proportion of added value is shown in percentage. Thus, proportion of added value and vertical integration represent the total output of the company. Precondition for a reduction of the vertical integration is the outsourcing of products which have so far been produced internallyto external suppliers. Thus, the company achieves a higher flexibility and can profit from specialised suppliers, which can in turn create competitive advantages. Furthermore, production processes will be less complex. Especially, the administration of production planning and materials management will be simplified.[116]

---

[114] cf. Arnold, (Beschaffungsmanagement), p. 13.
[115] cf. Weber, (Wertschöpfungsrechnung), p. 36.
[116] cf. Corsten, (Lexikon der Betriebswirtschaftslehre), p. 1031 – 1036.

IV. List of References

ARIBA Inc. (Ed.), (2004): Solutions Overview, Online in the Internet:
http://www.ariba.com/solutions/solutions_overview.cfm
(Status 05.06.2004; call-off 05.06.2004).

Arnold, Ulli: Beschaffungsmanagement, Stuttgart, 1995.

Arnolds, Hans/Heege, Franz/Tussing, Werner: Materialwirtschaft und Einkauf:
praxisorientiertes Lehrbuch, 10. Auflage, Wiesbaden, 2001.

Bichler, Klaus: Beschaffungs- und Lagerwirtschaft, Wiesbaden, 2001.

Bloech, Jürgen/Rottenbacher, Stefan: Materialwirtschaft: Kostenanalyse,
Ergebnisdarstellung und Planungsansätze, Stuttgart, 1986.

BMW Group (Ed.), (2003): Geschäftsbericht 2000: Produktion und Beschaffung,
Online in the Internet:
http://www.bmwgroup.com/d/nav/index.html?http://www.bmwgroup.com/d/0
_0_www_bmwgroup_com/2_investor_relations/2_2_publikationen/2_2_1_ge
schaeftsbericht_00/2_2_1_3_inalt_gb_00/2_2_1_3_3_konzern/2_2_1_3_3_5
_produktion.shtml (Status 28.09.2003; call-off 05.06.2004)

Bogaschewsky, Ronald (Ed.): Elektronischer Einkauf: Erfolgspotenziale.
Praxisanwendungen, Sicherheits- und Rechtsfragen, in: BME-Expertenreihe
vol. 4, Gernsbach, 1999.

Buchholz, Wolfgang/Bach, Norbert: The Evolution of Netsourcing business models
: Learning from the Past and Exploiting Future Opportunities, in:
Arbeitspapier der Professur BWL II, Prof. Dr. W. Krüger, Justus-Liebig-
Universität Gießen, 2001, p 5.

Corsten, Hans (Ed.): Lexikon der Betriebswirtschaftslehre, 4th Ed., München –
Wien – Oldenbourg, 2000.

Dobler, Donald W./Burt, David N: Purchasing and supply Management: text and
cases, New York, 1996.

Dolmetsch, Ralph: eProcurement: Sparpotential im Einkauf, 1st Ed., München,
2001.

Dyer, Jeffrey, H./Chu, Wujin: The determinants of trust in supplier-automaker
relationships in the US, Japan and Korea, in: Journal of international business
studies (Ed.), vol. 31, Detroit, Mich., 2000, p. 259-285.

ECIN (Ed.), (2003): Beschaffung: eProcurement und Outsourcing gehen Hand in Hand, Online in the Internet: http://www.ecin.de/news/2003/11/04/06390/ (Status 31.07.2003; call-off 11.05.2004).

Femerling, Christian. : Strategische Auslagerungsplanung, Wiesbaden, 1997.

Friedl, Birgit: Grundlagen des Beschaffungscontrolling, Berlin 1990; Diss., Tübingen, 1989.

Grochla, Erwin/Schönbohm, Peter: Beschaffung in der Unternehmung: Einführung in eine umfassende Beschaffungslehre, Stuttgart, 1980.

Hammann, Peter/Lohrberg, Werner: Beschaffungsmarketing: eine Einführung, Stuttgart, 1996.

Hartmann, Eva: Successful Indroduction of B2B Electronic Marketplace Projects, Diss., Berlin, 2002, p. 12f.

Hohaus, Wolfram: Zehn vor zwölf für den Einkauf, in: Diebold Management Report (Ed.), paper 10, 1999, p. 8.

Horchler, Hartmut: Outsourcing: eine Analyse der Nutzung und ein Handbuch der Umsetzung, Köln, 2001.

iMPOWER (Ed.),(2003): Purchasing Cards, Online in the Internet: http://www.nepp.org.uk/80256d8900466fd6/httppublicassets/79c0e77ea7997e4380256db20046cd6e/$file/technical+overview+-+purchasing+cards.pdf (Status 10.01.2003; call-off 08.06.2004).

InformationWeek (Ed.), (2000): E-Procurement – BMW geht eigene Wege, Online in the Internet: http://www.informationweek.de/index.php3?/channels/channel08/001440b.htm, (Status 02.06.2000; call-off 05.06.2004).

Kaup, Marcel, wallmedien AG (2003): eProcurement-Systeme im Einsatz, Online in the Internet: http://www.ecin.de/strategie/healthcare/print.html (Status 31.07.2003; call-off11.05.2004).

Kersten, Wolfgang: Geschäftsmodelle und Perspektiven des industriellen Einkaufs im Electronic Business, in: ZfB-Ergänzungsheft (Ed.), vol. 3, Wiesbaden, 2001, p. 21-37.

Köhler-Frost, Wilfried (Ed.)/Baaken, Thomas: Outsourcing – Eine strategische Allianz besonderen Typs, 2nd Ed., Berlin, 1995.

Koppelmann, Udo: Outsourcing, Stuttgart, 1996.

Laforsch, Matthias/Mielke, Adrian, BearingPoint GmbH (2003): Das Outsourcing Momentum nutzen, Online in the Internet: http://www.logistik-inside.de/sixcms4/sixcms_upload/media/1073/laforsch_neu1.pdf), (Status 01.07.2003; call-off 05.06.2004).

Lippmann, Herbert: Beschaffungsmarketing: Grundlagen einer einzelwirtschaftlich-funktionalen Beschaffungslehre, Bielefeld, 1980.

Manager-magazin.de (Ed.), (2003): Daimler-Projekt: Rückschlag für HP, Online in the Internet: http://rs.net-hh.de/ebusiness/artikel/0,2828,275926,00.html (Status 28.11.2003; call-off 07.06.2004).

Meinhold, Jens/Grobla, Mario, Siemens AG (2004): Outtasking schafft neue Handlungsspielräume, Online in the Internet: http://www.ecin.de/strategie/outtasking/print.html (Status 13.05.2004; call-off 19.05.2004).

Müller, Dietmar, CNET Networks Inc. (2003): HP verliert Outsourcing-Deal mit DaimlerChrysler, Online in the Internet: http://www.zdnet.de/news/business/0,39023142,39117851,00.htm (Status 28.11.2003; call-off 08.06.2004).

Pulic, Armin (Ed.), (2003): Aktuelle Trends in der Beschaffung indirekter Materialen, Online in the Internet: http://www.procurementletter.de/archiv/2003/pL-122003.pdf (Status 11.12.2003; call-off 28.05.2004).

Reichmann, Thomas/Palloks Monika: Make-or-Buy-Kalkulationen im modernen Beschaffungsmanagement, in: Hahn, Dietger/Kaufmann, Lutz (Ed.): Handbuch Industrielles Beschaffungsmanagement – internationale Konzepte – innovative Instrumente – aktuelle Praxisbeispiele, Wiesbaden, 1999, p. 419-421.

Roland, Folker: Beschaffungsstrategien: Vorraussetzungen, Methoden und EDV-Unterstützung einer problemadäquaten Auswahl, Bergisch Gladbach, 1993; Diss., Göttingen, 1993.

Sawall, Achim, Internet.com (2004): Daimler-Chrysler beerdigt Plan alle Desktop-PCs von nur einem Zulieferer zu beziehen, Online in the Internet: http://de.internet.com/index.php?id=2028738 (Status 28.05.2004; call-off 08.06.2004).

Schanz, Günther: Organisationsgestaltung: Management von Arbeitsteilung und
   Koordination, 2nd Ed., München, 1994.

Schneider, Dirk/Schnetkamp, Gerd: E-Markets : B2B-Strategien im Electronic
   Commerce: Marktplätze, Fachportale, Plattformen, 1st Ed., Wiesbaden, 2000.

Schneider, Hermann: Outsourcing von Beschaffungsprozessen:
   Beschaffungsdienstleister und ihre Konzepte, in: BME-Expertenreihe (Ed.)
   vol. 2, Gernsheim, 1998, p. 9-22.

Seeger, Heinrich. (2003): Desktop-Outsourcing bei DaimlerChrysler – Riesen
   Transfer mit Riesen Risiko, Online in the Internet:
   http://www.cio.de/index.cfm?PageID=300&cat=det&maid=2894&aid=3
   (Status 03.11.2003; call-off 07.06.2004).

Stangl, Ulrich: Beschaffungsmarkforschung – ein heuristisches
   Entscheidungsmodell, 2nd Ed., Köln, 1988.

Tripp, Horst: Electronic Procurement Services, Lohmar, 2002; Diss., St. Gallen,
   2002.

Universität Kitzbühel (Ed.), (2003): New challenges in the Automotive Industry,
   in: Laforsch, M/Mielke, A., BearingPoint GmbH (2003): Das Outsourcing
   Momentum nutzen, Online in the Internet: http://www.logistik-
   inside.de/sixcms/sixcms_upload/media/1073/laforsch_neu1.pdf),
   (Status 01.07.2003; call-off 05.06.2004).

Walser, Michael/Zimmer, Andreas: E-procurement: C-Teile Beschaffung via
   Internet, in series: Leitfaden E-Business 5, PWC, Dreieich, 1999 or: ibid,
   (1999): Online in the Internet: http://www.pwcglobal.com/de/ger/ins-
   sol/publ/ger_510_089_05.pdf (Status 1999; call-off 27.05.2004).

Warnecke, Hans-Jürgen: Die Fraktale Fabrik – Revolution der Unternehmenskultur,
   Berlin, 1992.

Weber, Jürgen: Alternative Organisationskonzepte der betrieblichen
   Datenverarbeitung, in: Heinzl, Armin/Weber, Jürgen (Ed.): Alternative
   Organisationskonzepte der betrieblichen Datenverarbeitung, Stuttgart, 1993,
   p. 6-38.

Womack, James P./Jones, Daniel T./Roos, Daniel: Die zweite Revolution in der
   Autoindustrie: Konsequenzen aus der weltweiten Studie aus dem
   Massachusetts Institute of Technology, 8th Ed., Frankfurt am Main, 1994.